To Diane—I am grateful that we met on a mindful path.

FJS

First published in Great Britain in 2023 by Singing Dragon,
an imprint of Jessica Kingsley Publishers
An Hachette Company

1

Front cover image source: Lily Fossett.

A CIP catalogue record for this title is available from
the British Library and the Library of Congress

ISBN 978 1 83997 679 7
eISBN 978 1 83997 680 3

Printed and bound in China by Leo Paper Products Ltd

Jessica Kingsley Publishers' policy is to use papers that
are natural, renewable and recyclable products and
made from wood grown in sustainable forests. The
logging and manufacturing processes are expected
to conform to the environmental regulations of the
country of origin.

Jessica Kingsley Publishers
Carmelite House
50 Victoria Embankment
London EC4Y 0DZ

www.singingdragon.com

Zensations

**Frank J. Sileo &
Christopher Willard**

Illustrated by Lily Fossett

SINGING DRAGON

LONDON AND PHILADELPHIA

You may think **ZENSATIONS** is a funny word.
It's probably something that you've never heard.

But what *are* zensations, I know you might say.
They're **bodily feelings**, which you feel each day.

Zensations are felt from your head to your toes—
In places between, like your chest and your nose.

Zensations are also **clues** to how you are feeling.
Checking in with your body can be quite revealing.

A **warmish** red face may mean we're upset.
When we get too worried, sometimes we may sweat.

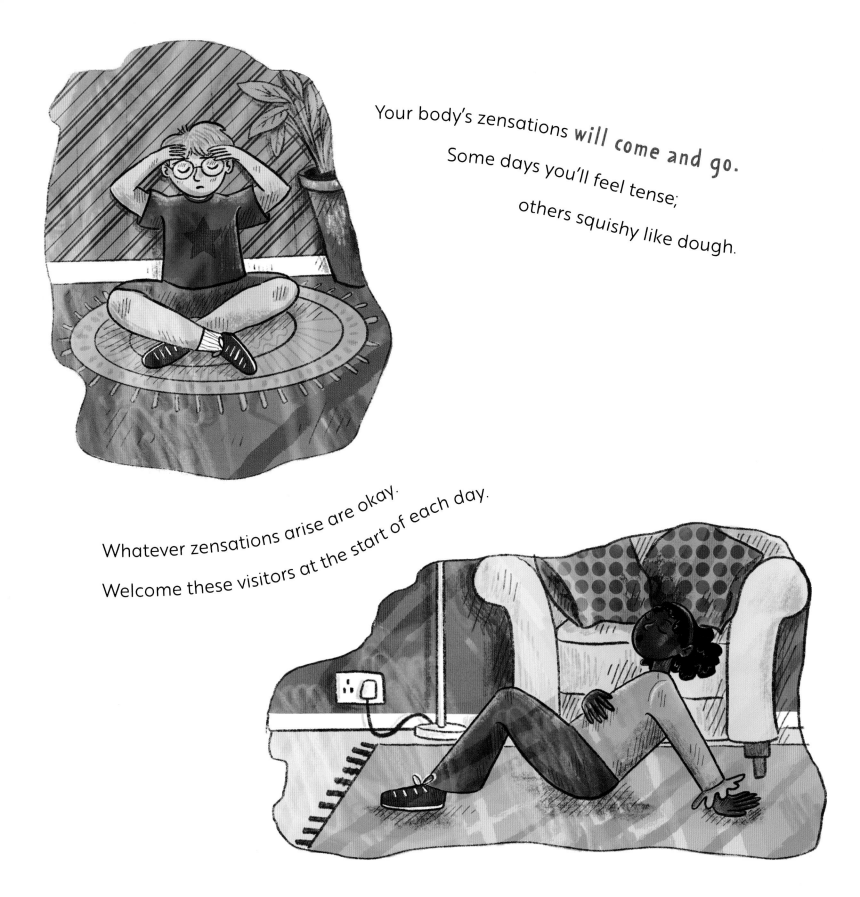

Your body's zensations **will come and go.**
Some days you'll feel tense;
others squishy like dough.

Whatever zensations arise are okay.
Welcome these visitors at the start of each day.

To feel our zensations, let's try something new:
A full **body scan** is what we can do.

A body scan helps make your zensations clear,
Bringing attention to calmness or fear.

Body scans work any time of the day,
To **notice your feelings** and send stress away.

So, why are you waiting? Should we do a scan?
A **comfy position** is first, if you can.

Sit in a chair or lie down on a bed.
Loosen your body and go rest your head.

You can close your eyes, but that isn't required.
Or leave them open if you start to feel tired.

Take a deep breath in, then let it out slow.
Is your exhale long or short? Just **let it flow.**

Now that you're ready, let's start with your feet.
What do you feel? Is it coolness or heat?

Move to the bottom of your foot and heel.
What other zensations can you **start to feel?**

Touching the base of your feet may cause giggles.

How does it feel to give your toes some wiggles?

Next, twirl your ankles around and around.

Lie quietly without making a sound.

Move to your legs now, and **notice** them there.
Do they feel heavy or light like the air?

Turn your awareness to one or both knees.
Breathe in, breathe out. Feel a new **sense of ease.**

A bit further up, bring your **mind** to your tummy.
Is it rumbling around like you ate something yummy?

Take a deep breath; feel it rise up and fall.
Your breath does the work. **You do nothing at all.**

Now let's move higher, up into your chest.
Feel the zensations when it is at rest.

Take a deep breath in, then **hold and release.**
Are there zensations? Can you feel any peace?

Moving through your body, **staying on track**,
What are the zensations there in your back?

As your back meets the bed or the chair,
What can you feel from the clothes that you wear?

Shift to your shoulders now. How do they feel?
What do the zensations inside them **reveal?**

Notice your arms, and your wrists, hands and fingers.
Is there a zensation in there that just lingers?

Fingers spread wide; then curl in a fist.
Let go of the tension. Now swirl your wrist.

Notice your neck; move it left and then right.
Does it feel loose **today**, or does it feel tight?

Move your way up to your head and your face.
This is where many zensations take place.

Notice your mouth. Is it wet now or dry?
What do you feel when you **smile?** Go on, try!

Now bring **attention** on up to your eyes.
Any zensations catch you by surprise?

Scrunch up your forehead and your eyes, as well!
Relax. What's the difference? Can you tell?

Feel your whole body; the scan is now done.
Continue exploring; we hope you had fun!

Now you know what body scans are about.
Is there a zensation that really stood out?

Zensations are special; you know that it's true.
You're special, too—**a zensational you!**

NOTE TO CAREGIVERS

This book was inspired by a mindfulness practice called "The Body Scan," which can help people become more aware of and appreciate their body. It may seem strange, but often if we pay more attention to how our body feels in a mindful way, unpleasant sensations actually bother us less. Ideally, we begin to notice that discomfort comes and goes in terms of how the body feels, and the story we tell ourselves about our body is not always accurate. Over time, we learn about our reactions to our body and its messages. We may also start to see that, like physical feelings, emotions also come and go, and are often more complex and even tolerable than we think at first.

As you practice with your child, they may begin to notice all kinds of emotions in different parts of the body. Mad, sad and even glad feel different and live in different places, as well as many other emotions, too. We encourage you to watch these come and go as well, and listen to your body for what it's telling or asking you in terms of what it needs or wants. This practice can be done any time of the day. As long as difficult emotions and sensations do not arise, it can be an excellent bedtime ritual.

We hope that you and your child find the book helpful as they learn to appreciate their body and how helpful it is to all aspects of their life. Lastly, if difficult thoughts, feelings or memories come up around your child's body or parts of their body, it's important for them to talk to a trustworthy adult about the experience.

These questions might be helpful to guide insight as you read the book and afterwards:

- ☀ What feelings do you notice in what parts of your body?

- ☀ What are the words that you would use to describe the different sensations in your body?

- ☀ How long do sensations and emotions tend to last in your body?

- ☀ Did any sensation surprise you?

- ☀ Were there any sensations you enjoyed?

- ☀ Were there any that you disliked?

The Lie That Wasn't
Big Things Happen When Little
Lies Come True...
Sarah Naish
Illustrated by Lily Fossett
ISBN 978 1 83997 372 7
eISBN 978 1 83997 373 4

The Red Beast
Helping Children on the Autism
Spectrum to Cope with Angry Feelings
K.I. Al-Ghani
Illustrated by Haitham Al-Ghani
ISBN 978 1 83997 275 1
eISBN 978 1 83997 276 8

The A–Z of Therapeutic Parenting
Strategies and Solutions
Sarah Naish
ISBN 978 1 78592 376 0
eISBN 978 1 78450 732 9

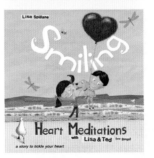

**Smiling Heart Meditations with
Lisa and Ted (and Bingo)**
Lisa Spillane
ISBN 978 1 84819 200 3
eISBN 978 0 85701 168 8

Frank J. Sileo, PhD is a licensed psychologist, international speaker and multi-award-winning author of 15 children's picture books, including four on mindfulness practices. He also wrote an award-winning parenting book that deals with raising chronically medically ill children. Since 2010, he has been consistently recognized as one of New Jersey's top kids' doctors. Dr. Sileo has had his research published in psychological journals, and is often a go-to psychologist in the media. He lives in New Jersey and is an avid I Love Lucy collector. Visit drfranksileo.com and on Facebook, Twitter and Instagram @DrFrankSileo.

Christopher Willard, PsyD is a clinical psychologist, author and consultant based in Massachusetts. He has spoken in 30 countries and has presented at two TEDx events. He is the author of 20 books, including *Growing Up Mindful* (2016), *Breathing Makes it Better* (2019) and *Alphabreaths Too* (2022). He has two kids and teaches at Harvard Medical School.

Lily Fossett is an illustrator based in Bath and a recent graduate of Falmouth University! She has a passion for creating character-led children's illustrations and uses digital media and textures to produce her work. Storytelling has always been a key focus of Lily's, and she loves to capture and evoke emotion in her drawings. The natural world is also a large inspiration and is often a focus within her colorful illustrations.